Original title:
The Current of Forever

Copyright © 2025 Creative Arts Management OÜ
All rights reserved.

Author: Finn Donovan
ISBN HARDBACK: 978-1-80587-447-8
ISBN PAPERBACK: 978-1-80587-917-6

The Embrace of Eternity

In a world where time is bent,
People trip on hours spent.
We dance with clocks, a silly show,
Laughing as the minutes go.

We wear our watches on our feet,
And ask for time on bathroom sheets.
With every tick, a goofy grin,
Embracing chaos, let's begin!

When seconds stretch like silly putty,
And urgency feels quite corny and nutty.
We twirl through days, a merry band,
Waving goodbye to time's command.

As night falls, we lose our track,
Chasing dreams, there's no way back.
Eternity's laughs, a playful rhyme,
We'll be silly every time!

Whispering Waters

Streams giggle under the sun,
Puddle-jumpers, oh what fun!
Waterfalls spill secrets so bright,
While fish perform to our delight.

Raindrops tap dance on leaves,
Singing songs only nature believes.
With every splash, a chuckle's found,
As frogs croak jokes, quite profound.

Ripples spread like laughter's cheer,
In the brook, we shed our fear.
We float along, paddling with glee,
With the current's grin, we just may be free.

So heed the whispers of water's cheer,
In every wave, there's joy so near.
We'll ride the tide, forever merry,
Chasing mirth like a cherry berry!

Tracing Circles in Time

We draw round patterns in the sand,
And giggle as they slip from hand.
With every spin, we lose our place,
Time's a doodle, a funny race.

A clock with legs walks away,
Chasing moments, it can't stay.
Each tick-tock a laugh, a wink,
Forget the past! It's gone in a blink.

We trace our steps in endless loops,
Zigzagging like a flock of goofs.
With every turn and tumble down,
We gather laughs, not a frown.

Though paths may twist and twirl about,
Life's a circle with no room for doubt.
We dance in spirals, round and round,
Time's silly game shall ever abound!

The Melodies of Forever

Tunes of laughter fill the air,
With notes that wiggle everywhere.
We sing off-key, just like a pro,
In this grand show, we steal the show!

The wind hums a silly tune,
As butterflies sway to the moon.
Each chirp and giggle makes us sway,
Turning our troubles into play.

Melodies drift on waves of cheer,
With every strum, our hearts draw near.
Playing jokes like a funny band,
Strumming fate with a wobbly hand.

In this symphony, we forget the score,
Laughing louder, we always want more.
So join the chorus, sing and swing,
In the dance of jest, we are kings!

The Vastness of Endless Blue

In a pool of thought, the ducks float by,
Wearing tiny hats, they reach for the sky.
Fish hold their breath, avoiding a glance,
While frogs do a jig, in their own kind of dance.

Clouds play tag with the sun's warm rays,
While laughter echoes in silly ways.
Seagulls squawk jokes that make waves laugh,
Mermaids sell seashells, their ghosts do the math.

Whirlwinds of the Ever-Present

The wind is a prankster, a jester in flight,
Tickling the trees, making leaves dance with delight.
It sneaks up behind like a playful old friend,
Laughing out loud, it refuses to end.

Kites soar high, in a tangle of strings,
Chasing the clouds, oh, the joy that it brings!
Children chase shadows that play hide and seek,
While ice cream melts down, leaving sticky cheeks.

The Unfathomable Stream

A river of giggles flows past the line,
Where pebbles tell stories, both silly and fine.
Rabbits in boats wear flamboyant attire,
While turtles play poker, fueled by desire.

Once, a fish proclaimed, 'I'm the king of this stream!'
But he tripped on a twig and fell with a scream.
Otters threw parties on shores of soft sand,
Bouncing on waves like they're in a band.

Navigating the Sea of Time

Watch clocks swim backward beneath the moonlight,
Ticking in rhythm, they tease and ignite.
Sailors with umbrellas, tossed backwards on waves,
Chasing their watches like playful knaves.

Time's a big jester with stories to tell,
Riding on dolphins, they yodel and yell.
With whirlpool giggles, they spin 'round and round,
Hoping that laughter is always profound.

Timeless Connections

In a world where clocks are rude,
A cat naps deep, with dreams quite lewd.
Time forgot his coffee break,
Yet, here we are, for goodness' sake!

The fish in tanks have endless chats,
While squirrels plan their acrobat flats.
A toaster burns some bread quite bright,
Cheering us on in the morning light.

Jellybeans stuck in my hair,
Ask me how I got them there!
With every giggle and silly jest,
Friendship's the joke that we love best.

As whispers ride on dandelion seeds,
We thank the grass for all its deeds.
A moment shared is a moment won,
So let's make life a silly pun!

Driftwood Dreams

Floating past in a wooden shoe,
Where seaweed sings a tuneless tune.
The tides are wrecking all my plans,
As mermaids giggle in their bands.

Starfish have a dance-off at night,
While dolphins show off their best flight.
A clam decides to start a band,
Shell-shocked, we listen on the sand.

In dreams of sandcastles aglow,
We crown ourselves in the morning show.
Seagulls squawk with such delight,
Wondering who'll join the seagull fight.

So pack your dreams in a bottle deep,
And let the ocean make you leap.
Each wave that comes, a slap on the back,
Reminds us how absurd is our track!

Symphony of Unending Days

Pigeons coo in perfect sync,
While ants form lines to share a drink.
The sun hums tunes of lazy rays,
In this endless, funny ballet.

A grasshopper with fancy shoes,
Dances beneath the morning hues.
Time forgot to bring its hat,
So it joins in our silly chat.

Clouds wearing socks on their big feet,
Vote for the best dance on the street.
The wind gets tangled in a kite,
As laughter fills the day and night.

We march to rhythms, none too clear,
Each heartbeat echoes far and near.
A symphony of laughter plays,
In our topsy-turvy outdoor maze!

Threads of Cosmic Time

With threads of fate all in a tangle,
The universe loves a good wrangle.
Stars sneeze dust in a perfect arc,
While comets spark like a silly lark.

Planets trip on cosmic vines,
Arguing over salad lines.
Each twinkle holds a little joke,
As Saturn laughs and Venus pokes.

Galaxies spin in dizzy whirls,
While black holes giggle, stealing pearls.
Time throws confetti with each tick,
And space dances to a wobbly flick.

Each moment spins a yarn so grand,
In the tapestry of this strange land.
With every joke and playful rhyme,
Life's a quilt sewn in cosmic time!

Among the Endless Streams

In a river where socks swim free,
And fish dance with glee, oh me!
I once saw a frog wear a crown,
He ruled the pond with a goofy frown.

Ducks quack jokes that make them float,
While turtles argue who's the best quote.
The grasshoppers strike up a band,
Playing tunes on a lily pad stand.

Raccoons host dinners with pies of mud,
And mice juggle crumbs with a heartthrob thud.
The otters slide down with epic flair,
Rolling in laughter, no worries, no care.

So join in this party, don't be shy,
We'll toast to the clouds in the sky.
With giggles and wiggles, we'll always roam,
In this wacky world, we've all found home.

Reflections on a Boundless Surface

A mirror on water, the ducks say hi,
Reflecting their dance, oh my, oh my!
The fish wear sunglasses, swimming in style,
Making the sea turtles crack a sly smile.

The sun winks at clouds, swirling around,
While the wind plays tag without making a sound.
Raindrops join in, a splashy ballet,
As puddles become dance floors for the day.

A crab writes poetry, in sand with a claw,
While a snail, in a hurry, just scoffs in awe.
The laughter erupts from a clam in a shell,
He's hiding a secret; it's just as well.

In this world of reflections, we giggle and play,
At the edge of the pond, we waste not a day.
With splashes and sparkles that twinkle and gleam,
We find joy together in a whimsical dream.

The Voyage Past Time's Edge

Set sail on a boat made of toast,
As jellyfish sing, we dance and boast.
Time is a trickster, always in flight,
But snack break first, it feels so right!

With sandwiches tossed like confetti in air,
The seagulls reply with a sassy flair.
We're pirates of whimsy, with treasure of fun,
Each adventure a laugh, under the sun.

Navigating waters where giggles collide,
With mermaids who surf on hot dog slides.
The clocks on the shore are melting like cheese,
In this bizarro world, we do what we please.

So grab a cap, let's spin in a whirl,
On this voyage of laughter, let happiness unfurl.
Time can't catch us; we're faster than light,
Just remember to smile, it's a wondrous flight.

Unfurling the Layers of Existence

Like onions of laughter, we peel back the skin,
Beneath each layer, there's joy to win.
With every slice, a giggle escapes,
In this zany world of clownish shapes.

The apples are dancing, a merry delight,
While bananas juggle, oh what a sight!
The carrots debate who's the crunchiest prize,
With radishes laughing at their own lies.

With cupcakes debating, should sprinkles be mesh,
Chocolate chips tumble, oh what a mess!
Pie crusts are clamoring for a sweet role,
While whipped cream tops just take a stroll.

As we unfurl layers, uncovering dreams,
We find that existence is wilder than schemes.
In a banquet of giggles, let's feast, go ahead,
For life is a party, joyfully spread.

Echoes of an Endless Journey

I packed my bags, forgot my hat,
The map was upside down, imagine that!
With snacks in hand, I hit the road,
But tripped on my laces, oh what a load!

While chasing sunsets, I lost my shoe,
But hey, who needs feet to enjoy the view?
The stars above laughed, shining bright,
I danced in circles, what a silly sight!

A hitchhiker waved, said 'need a ride?'
I told him I would, if he could provide!
A cloud, a dream, or a talking frog,
I'd trade my pizza for a fortune dog!

So here's to travels, the laughs, the waits,
To roads unknown, and bizarre fates!
With giggles and snickers, we carry on,
Together forever, till the break of dawn!

Liquid Memories

Splashing puddles of laughter, we run,
The rain's a dance, oh, such silly fun!
Umbrellas flipping like fish at sea,
I caught one flying, it just won't be!

Sipping our cocoa, mustache in tow,
We tripped on a marshmallow, oh no, oh no!
Memories swirl in a chocolate dream,
We giggle and snort, what a sticky theme!

In this little pond of whipped cream delight,
We'd swim with spoons, in the moon's soft light!
The waves of giggles ripple all around,
Here's where sweet chaos happily is found!

So grab a floatie, let's drift on by,
With whipped topping skies, we will surely fly!
We'll drown in laughter, together so bold,
As liquid memories pour, stories unfold!

The Tidepool of Days

A crab wore a hat, how absurd, I say,
Waving to fishes, 'Come join the play!'
Time's a slippery starfish, in constant flip,
Each moment we catch makes us giggle and slip!

Seashells whisper secrets of what they've seen,
'Yesterday's jellyfish danced like a queen!'
We measured our joy in tides of delight,
Tripping on seaweed, a comical sight!

With each rising wave, our laughter grows loud,
As seagulls squawk tunes, we're lost in the crowd!
The barnacles cheer for the moments we break,
In this tidepool of days, happiness we make!

So wade through the giggles, let worries float,
We'll sail through the chaos on a rubber boat!
For every splash we make, with friends by our side,
In this silly sea, our joy is our guide!

A Cascade of Timeless Dreams

Under the starlight, we chase our sights,
On a trampoline made of fluffy delights!
Melting ice cream falls from the sky,
As visions of cupcakes with sprinkles fly!

We ride on the breezes of whimsical tales,
As unicorns prance through gales of sails!
Dancing on rainbows, we twirl and swoon,
With marshmallow clouds, we float like a balloon!

Time's a jester, playing games with our hearts,
Each laugh, a treasure, as our story starts!
A tumble through twinkles, we wiggle and spin,
In a cascade of dreams, where the fun will begin!

So hop on this ride, with giggles and glee,
For today's little moments are crazy and free!
In a wacky world, we'll sing through the beams,
Forever enchanted in timeless dreams!

An Odyssey Without End

I set sail on a boat made of cheese,
With a crew of mice, doing just as they please.
Waves of pickle juice splash all around,
We laugh till we fall, then we bounce on the ground.

A pirate shows up with a parrot named Fred,
He demands all our snacks or we'll end up in bread.
We barter with crackers, a fine feast ahead,
And sail past the sunsets, in peace, it is said.

The stars are so bright, they twinkle and glow,
They dance on the waves, putting on quite a show.
I tried to catch one, but it slipped through my hands,
And landed on deck, where it started to dance.

So here we drift on, in this infinite spree,
With laughter and snacks, as wild as can be.
A journey so silly, it never will cease,
In a world made of bisque, we find all our peace.

Flowing Through Eternity

I once met a fish that wore a top hat,
He offered me tea, while I sat on a mat.
We talked about dreams, like flying to Mars,
While hopping on jellybeans and juggling stars.

Then came a turtle who claimed he could dance,
He twirled on a wave, gave the sea room to prance.
We cheered and we chuckled, his moves were quite bold,
As he slipped on some kelp — oh, the sight was pure gold!

The ocean giggled and splashed with delight,
As bubbles confided their secrets at night.
We crafted a boat of laughter and song,
And sailed through the laughter, where nothing feels wrong.

So off we go, in this silly parade,
With friends made of bubbles, in the sun's warm cascade.
We'll shimmy forever, with stories to share,
In a whimsical journey, with giggles to spare.

Ripples of the Unfathomable

A jellyfish juggler named Larry we found,
Played tricks with his tentacles, twirling around.
He forgot how to swim, but that's just his style,
He floated on laughter, and giggled awhile.

A clam gave a wink, and it startled us all,
As it challenged the seagull to a dance-off ball.
They flapped and they clacked, feathers flew everywhere,
While fish rolled their eyes, breathing bubbles of air.

The tide did its dance, a gentle ballet,
Swirling us round in an underwater sway.
With starfish applauding, it was quite the show,
As the sea turned into a grand circus flow.

So we bop through the waves, where the ripples take hold,
With friends made of seaweed, and laughter so bold.
In this oceanic saga, let the fun never cease,
As we ride the absurd, in waves of pure peace.

Journey Beyond the Shore

I packed up my sandals, my kite, and some snacks,
A map made of candy, but alas, no tracks.
With seagulls as guides, we took off with a cheer,
To a land where the sun always shines bright and clear.

We stumbled on crabs, who wore sunglasses cool,
They played tiny fiddles and skipped by the pool.
I tried to join in, but I tripped on a shell,
And fell in a splash, oh, I laughed like a bell.

The sandcastles chatted, with turrets so grand,
They even gave tours, all built on the sand.
We raced with the breeze, hopped from dune to dune,
In a parade of sunbeams, while humming a tune.

As the stars peeked out, we waved our goodbye,
To the silliness wrapped in the night sky so high.
With hearts full of joy, and stories galore,
We'll bounce back to shore, then set off for more!

The Waves of Wistfulness

In a sea of socks, lost and found,
Tumbling through the laundry round.
Thoughts of dolphins sipping tea,
While fish skateboards under the sea.

Crabby crabs with choreographed moves,
Dance the night away in grooves.
A whale tells jokes, but no one hears,
Laughter floats through the salty tears.

Seagulls wear hats; they think they're fly,
With shades and beaks up to the sky.
Mermaids giggle, swapping tales,
As jellyfish get caught in gales.

All these thoughts in waves collide,
Making smiles, a joyful tide.
Each wave's a chuckle, soft and grand,
In this ocean, nothing's planned.

In the Heart of Evermore

In a land where time forgot to tick,
Socks grow legs and suddenly stick.
Cats wear capes and chase their tails,
While fish recount their underwater tales.

Teapots whistle tunes of yore,
As ghosts play poker by the door.
A stork delivers pies, oh what a sight,
In a world where wrong is always right.

Birds recite Shakespeare with flair,
While rabbits debate from their armchair.
Umbrellas dance in the afternoon sun,
This whimsical world is just pure fun.

And over the hills, giggles resound,
While marshmallows float, gummy bears abound.
Each moment's a sketch, a laugh, a cheer,
In this heart where joy's always near.

Streams of Ceaseless Wonder

A river flows through silly dreams,
With fish who plot their daring schemes.
A turtle spins a yarn so fast,
While frogs debate who's best at jazz.

Butterflies wear hats made of cheese,
Sipping nectar, aiming to please.
Rain drops hum like a playful tune,
As flowers boogie beneath the moon.

Each pebble holds a secret laugh,
While ants map routes to the crazy half.
Snails in shades crawl at their own pace,
In this stream, life's a curious race.

And so we dance on waters bright,
Where giggles echo day and night.
Every splash can turn to a show,
In the stream where wonders flow.

Boundless Horizons

On the edge of the world, the sun winks wide,
Clouds put on ruffles, take a wild ride.
Kangaroos wear vests of plaid and stripes,
Debating if they'd rather be types.

Mountains wear glasses, oh what a view,
As squirrels plot antics, a crazy crew.
A parade of ants with tiny drums,
Marching along, while everyone hums.

Balloons float by, chatting with trees,
Tickling leaves in the gentle breeze.
Stars comically wink, "Here we are!"
Reminding us all, we're never too far.

With horizons that stretch beyond the night,
Every dream takes flight with delight.
In laughter's embrace, we boldly roam,
In this world, we always feel at home.

Resonance of the Lifeforce

In the dance of quirky stars,
We giggle and chase with Mars.
Elves confuse a cat for a deer,
Prancing with glee, it's all very clear.

When socks escape the laundry's grasp,
We find them in an odd, warm clasp.
Life hums along in goofy tones,
While toasters pop and munch on scones.

Balloons take flight in a comical breeze,
Chasing giggles with utmost ease.
Frogs in tuxedos jump away,
Singing, "Come join our cabaret!"

So here we dance in silly cheer,
Embracing quirks that we all hold dear.
A tapestry of laughter and mirth,
In every corner of our Earth.

Time's Soft Embrace

Tick-tock chuckles, clocks in disguise,
With mustaches and ruddy eyes.
Each second winks, a playful tease,
Inviting us to dance with ease.

Muffins sit in a wordy debate,
About the best time to elevate.
While friends in pajamas throw confetti,
Chasing moments, oh so petty!

Whiskers twitch, a cat plays ball,
While dogs conspire to make us fall.
As hours 'round corners like jesters peek,
"Are we too early, or just a freak?"

So let's embrace the time we share,
In this whimsy we lovingly wear.
Laughter's the clock that'll never slow,
In joys that only we can bestow.

The Unfurling of Infinite Paths

A squirrel wearing glasses reads a map,
While loading nuts into a cap.
Left or right? Oh, what a sight!
Pathways twinkle in the moonlight.

Puddles ripple with secrets new,
As gumdrops sprout where daisies grew.
The sun throws shade with a wink and grin,
While hedgehogs hold poker games to win.

With wildflowers dancing on each trail,
And starlit lanterns, we humor our fail.
Life's a choice between cake and pie,
Both slice at once, oh me, oh my!

In every twist and silly ways,
We play hopscotch through sunny rays.
Each step unfolds with laughter's cheer,
In paths we take, we tread without fear.

Ebb and Flow of the Unsung

The tide sings jokes that fish can't tell,
While crabs in bow ties jig and swell.
A dolphin flips with laughter bright,
And seaweed sways, keeping it light.

Waves tickle toes, as shells play tricks,
And mermaids scratch off bingo picks.
Jellyfish waltz in soft ballet,
As the lighthouse spins, shouting, "Hey!"

A whale hums tunes that make us grin,
While plankton dance as night begins.
The sea is a stage, and how we cheer,
With clams in hats and voices clear.

So here's a splash to those unseen,
The laughable wonders beneath the sheen.
Through ebb and flow, we'll always sing,
In waves of joy that life can bring.

The Timeless Voyage

In a boat made of cheese, we set off,
With a captain who laughs and a parrot that scoffs.
The waves are all giggles, the stars play along,
We sing silly sea shanties, all night long.

A sea monster waves, it's just a big cat,
Who's fishing for dreams while wearing a hat.
The compass spins wildly, it has lost its way,
But who needs direction when we're here to play?

Jellyfish dance like they're in a parade,
While seagulls compete in a dive-bomb charade.
The moon is a spotlight, for our grand show,
As we sail through the laughter, we frolic and flow.

Horizon of Perpetual Dawn

The sun is a jokester, pranking the stars,
With a daily routine of appearing from Mars.
The sky is a canvas, painted with glee,
As clouds wear pajamas and dance with a bee.

Tick-tock says the clock, but it can't keep pace,
With turtles who moonwalk in an infinite race.
Each moment's a chuckle, a tickle at best,
Who knew time could giggle and never need rest?

Sunflowers gossip, as meadows engage,
In a sitcom of nature, they're all on the stage.
The horizon's a joke that we won't forget,
In our laughter-filled world, we're never upset.

Waters of the Infinite

Splashing through puddles of giggly goo,
We paddle with spoons in a vibrant blue hue.
The fish tell tall tales, big as a house,
While ducks in tuxedos waltz with a mouse.

Raindrops are drummers in a jolly band,
Creating a ruckus, across the land.
The ripples are chuckling, the tide takes a bow,
A symphony of smiles is happening now.

Oceans wear pajamas, quite comfy indeed,
As jellybeans float, meeting every need.
With sunset confetti, the day wraps-up tight,
In these waters of fun, we dance through the night.

Stairway to Endlessness

Up the stairs made of giggles, we bounce and we leap,
Where echoes of laughter are treasures to keep.
Each step is a riddle, a prank in disguise,
With whoopee cushions making us cry from surprise.

Handrails of candy, how sweet they all are,
Leading us higher, up to a candy bar.
The land at the top is a cheeky delight,
With clouds made of marshmallows, fluffy and white.

Silly winds tickle our faces with cheer,
As we chase after dream-cakes that float ever near.
On this stairway to giggles, time slips like a toy,
In a world full of humor, we dance with pure joy.

Cascading into Eternity

In a river of socks, I float with glee,
Old rubber ducks join my wild spree.
Time wears a watch that's stuck at three,
Laughing at clocks as I sip my tea.

I tumbled down waterfalls made of cheese,
Riding the currents with whimsical ease.
Fish tell me jokes; they aim to please,
I chuckle so hard, I almost sneeze.

The sun wears sunglasses, glowing bright,
Bouncing on waves, oh what a sight!
Mermaids sing tunes all day and night,
In this crazy world of pure delight.

With jellyfish hats and shrimp on parade,
We dance through the chaos; I'm not afraid.
Tick-tock, tick-tock, but joy won't fade,
The soggy sock legends we all have made.

The Flow of Silent Dawns

Morning arrives with a belly flop,
The toast does a jig, and the kettle pops.
Socks on the ceiling, the milk never stops,
While the cat conducts symphonies, never drops.

Meanwhile, the sun think it's late for the game,
It dances with shadows — what a silly claim!
The world spins around like a wild spinning frame,
Chasing the laughter, never looking the same.

I ride on a butterfly's back, such a thrill,
It tickles my ribs as we glide down the hill.
Time plays a trick, what a mischievous quill,
Wishing for breakfast that's never quite real.

And then with a wink, the day starts to tease,
As the clock runs in circles, doing as it please.
If silly was wisdom, I'd bring it to knees,
In the flow of each dawn, where laughter's the keys.

Eternal Tides

Waves of giggles crash on the shore,
Sandcastles whisper, 'Build us some more!'
Seagulls are gossiping; they love to explore,
The secrets of fish who dance and adore.

As I wade in the tide, I trip on a shoe,
A crab calls to order, it's Monday, who knew?
Surfboards are plotting a mutiny too,
Against boring old sharks with their dull points of view.

Pineapple smoothies spill every hour,
While sunscreen battles the sun's mighty power.
With laughter that mixed all the sweet and sour,
We dance through the storms, oh what a flower!

Eternity giggles in bubbles of foam,
Where jellybeans fetch the best wishes to roam.
In tides of nonsense, we cheerfully comb,
With every horizon, we're back to our home.

Whispering Edges of Time

Tickling time with a feathered quill,
Thoughts float like clouds, too free to stand still.
A bumblebee's dance gives my heart a thrill,
As I ponder soft whispers that insist on the will.

The corners of moments are bending with cheer,
Upside-down wishes, all muddled, I fear.
But fortune cookies say, 'Your path's pretty clear,'
While jellybeans chase after my dear.

Twirling in circles, the hours just sing,
Like a giant balloon caught on a string.
Each giggle and chuckle has magic to bring,
Where whispers of time start to merrily swing.

So join me in jest as we dance through the haze,
In edges of laughter, we'll spend all our days.
With snickers and chuckles, let's set hearts ablaze,
In the land of the silly where we'll always amaze.

Lighthouses of an Endless Journey

The lighthouse winked, a cheeky glow,
Telling sailors, 'Hey, don't go slow!'
A seagull squawked, added to the fun,
With a beak full of fries—oh, tasty run!

Chasing waves, we danced on sand,
With jellyfish doing a conga band.
Our boat was a banana, it slipped and slid,
But laughter shone bright—how silly we did!

Waves like laughter, they crash and play,
Painting smiles as they come our way.
Tides had jokes, rising high and low,
We just rolled with it, go with the flow!

So here's to the lighthouses, bright and bold,
Guiding us through as the stories unfold.
An endless journey, lined with jest,
With every wave, we find our zest!

The Flowing Silence of Forever

In a quiet town, the crickets burst,
With jokes so bad, they almost thirst.
Whispers of wind, or so they claim,
But one squirrel said, 'I'm not to blame!'

A turtle raced, or so he swore,
While other folks took naps galore.
In the stillness, our giggles roam,
Bouncing 'round like a fluffy foam.

Echoes of laughter, like bubbles they rise,
A snail with shades under sunny skies.
Time stands still, but we don't care,
We're just here for the pranks to share.

So keep that silence, we'll make it loud,
In the calmest moments, we'll draw a crowd.
With smiles afloat, we drift and play,
In our flowing silence, we'll laugh all day!

Raindrops of Timeless Moments

Raindrops giggled as they hit the ground,
Each one a joke, not a single frown.
Puddles splashed, like puddles do,
With rubber ducks cheering, 'We've got you!'

Umbrellas turned inside out in the breeze,
When the clouds exploded, we just said 'Geez!'
A dance in the rain, a slip and a slide,
The more we fell, the more we tried!

Lightning flashed, with a wink and a tease,
'You call that a storm? I'll start with a sneeze!'
Windy whispers, like secrets told,
Every drop of laughter, pure and bold.

So here's to those moments, frozen in time,
With each raindrop dropping, we're in our prime.
Capture the giggles before they all fly,
In raindrops, we find joy soaring high!

Wandering Through the Infinite Veil

In a whimsical world, where socks mismatched,
A rabbit jumped by, and my shoe got scratched.
With tea leaves reading, what fate might hold,
'You'll meet a chicken!' the fortune told.

Lost in a maze of flowering words,
A parrot commented, 'You're for the birds!'
We wandered through giggles, and late-night chats,
With every turn found more silly hats.

The moon grinned down, a mischievous face,
As we stumbled forward, a laughable race.
Through foggy paths and sparkling dreams,
In every corner, a prank it seems.

So let's wander on, hand in hand,
Through jester's fields and laughter's strand.
In this infinite veil, forever we'll roam,
With each jokester's echo, we've built our home!

Flowing Dreams of Forever

In a river made of jelly, we float with glee,
Chasing rubber ducks and sipping sweet tea.
We dance with the fish and wear hats of cheese,
Laughter echoes like buzzing bumblebees.

Marmalade sun on our hopeful heads,
Ticklish waves where imagination treads.
A duck quacks jokes as it paddles away,
Time slips by like a well-worn play.

Tick tock goes the clock, full of whimsy,
Count the stars with a wink, oh so flimsy!
Hammocks swing dreams of being a spry,
We embrace the odd, let the silliness fly.

So let's chase our thoughts on a bubblegum breeze,
Holding hands with the clouds, feeling oh so at ease.
With every giggle, a memory is spun,
In a world where fun and dreams are never done.

Searching for the Unseen

With a magnifying glass, I scout the room,
Hunting for shadows that dance like a plume.
Nose in the air, I sniff out a clue,
Is it a mystery or old pizza, too?

The carpet's a jungle, my blanket a cape,
I'm the hero of chaos, no chance to escape.
My trusty sidekick is a cat named Fred,
Together we quest for the snacks we're fed.

Invisible beings with glittery shoes,
I call them my pals; they always amuse.
We plan a parade in an unseen realm,
But first must locate the last cookie's helm!

So here's to the unseen, the silly, the brief,
To absurd little whispers that steal away grief.
Searching and chuckling, what a splendid spree,
Life's just a game, and we're wild as can be!

Between Moments of Infinity

In the space between ticks of an ancient clock,
Time wears a hat that's made of tough rock.
I trip on the seconds while chasing a rhyme,
Slipping on giggles that dance out of time.

Teetering past dreams that float like a kite,
I wrangle with shadows in the pale moonlight.
Ice cream cone glasses, mismatched shoes too,
Here's a wink to the quirky; it's all tried-and-true.

In the squishy embrace of a marshmallow chair,
We gather our thoughts like floating down hair.
Sipping on laughter with a sprinkle of cheer,
Who knew that the unknown was so very near?

So let's hop on the path where the nonsense serves,
Between heartbeats and giggles, let's swerve.
With a sprinkle of whimsy, we'll navigate plays,
In this land of forever, we'll dance all our days.

Navigating the Vast Expanse

In a boat made of pizza, we sail on cheese seas,
Paddling with crayons, feeling the breeze.
Stars made of cupcakes twinkle with pride,
As we journey through dreams on this whimsical ride.

Worms in top hats keep us laughing aloud,
Navigating chaos with a wobbly crowd.
Balloons filled with giggles float high in the air,
We bounce on the waves without a single care.

Maps drawn with doodles and flavors of fun,
Charting out paths where the wild things run.
Exploring the corners of laughter and light,
Under skies painted silly with stars sparkling bright.

So let's cast our lines in the river of play,
Sailing through moments that dance our way.
With our sails full of dreams, we'll splatter the sky,
Navigating the vastness, letting laughter fly.

Everlasting Flow

In a river made of rubber ducks,
The fish wear hats and laugh at luck.
They float along in silly style,
While clowns on logs dance a while.

Bubbles burst with giggles loud,
As turtles try to join the crowd.
They slip and slide, such joyful cheer,
In waters that have no real fear.

Each wave is filled with laughter bright,
As seahorses take to flight!
They race the flow and always win,
A game they play with toothy grin.

So here we float on silly dreams,
Where nonsense reigns and laughter beams.
Life's just a splash of joyous play,
In a stream where fun won't decay.

The Cascade of Ages

In waterfalls of jellybeans,
The squirrels host their wacky scenes.
With candy crowns, they rule the land,
And guzzle lemonade so grand.

Old wisdom flows from frogs in togs,
Teaching yoga to lazy dogs.
They stretch and bark with all their might,
In a splash of joy, what a sight!

Every drop holds tales untold,
Of time itself, brightly bold.
With giggles stitched in every lane,
As time jumps on a sugar train.

Here laughter tumbles down like rain,
In a giddy, goofy, sweet refrain.
Through ages past, the fun won't stop,
As we each dance and spin and hop!

Unseen Lifelines

With strings of laughter tied so tight,
Invisible threads pull us to light.
A wink from fate, a nudge from chance,
We wear our quirks like a wild dance.

The shadows chat with floppy hats,
While squirrels host their dinner chats.
They snack on dreams, a tasty feast,
In a world where giggles never cease.

Each tread and stumble, a glorious bloop,
As disco party rules the troupe.
With every twirl, a silly slip,
Holding close our friendship grip.

Here's to silliness unseen,
A thread of joy, soft and keen.
So let us dance on life's bright line,
In laughter's grip, we'll always shine!

Continuum of Serendipity

In a world where cats can cook,
And dogs take books from every nook.
A serendipitous twist of fate,
Turns soup into cake on a plate!

Consider the fish who plays the sax,
While frogs strum ukes for fun little facts.
A disco ball made of spaghetti,
Leads the way to a pasta party ready!

Each moment spins in wild delight,
Where everything absurd feels just right.
Unexpected joy in every glance,
As shadows waltz and mischief prance.

So grab a snack and join the show,
To whims of wonders all aglow.
In this silly dance of fate's decree,
We find our place in jubilee!

Eternal Tides

Waves crash down with a cheeky grin,
A seagull steals my hot dog, where to begin?
I chase it down, flailing like a fool,
The ocean laughs as I jump in the pool.

Shells are hiding secrets, or so they claim,
I asked a starfish, but it played a game.
It tickled my toes, danced away in style,
The tide rolled in, oh, what a beguile!

Sandcastles crumble, a royal disgrace,
My moat's a puddle, can't keep up the pace.
The crab waves goodbye, pinches my shoe,
I'm just a beach bum, with nothing to do.

Time's a funny thing, it flies on a breeze,
I glance at my watch, oh please, just leave me at ease.
With every tick-tock, a laugh and a spin,
In this giggle of life, let the fun begin!

Whispers of Timeless Waves

The ocean whispers secrets, or so they say,
A dolphin told me jokes while I splashed in the bay.
I laughed so hard, water shot from my nose,
A clam rolled its eyes, and that's how it goes!

Turtles move slowly, but they're wise and slick,
They'll plan a heist, don't let them fool you quick.
I saw them plotting by a rock with a view,
In a game of shell poker, they knew how to chew.

The tides are a riddle, they pull and they push,
They tease the shoreline with a splash and a hush.
waves do the cha-cha, and I join the dance,
But sand in my shorts ruins the chance of romance.

Time tiptoes lightly on these wobbly floors,
While jellyfish tickle, and a crab's at the doors.
I'm caught in this whirlpool of laughter and fun,
As the hourglass spills, how can this be done?

Infinity in Motion

The clock's a jester, it laughs with a tick,
Saying 'don't worry, just get on with the trick!'
I tumble forward, I stumble back round,
Time's a merry-go-round spinning off the ground.

A squirrel in a tree gives a knowing look,
Checks his tiny watch, reads like a funny book.
"Hold on to your hat!" he giggles with glee,
As I chase after time, it's a wild jubilee!

The grass giggles under my dancing feet,
I step on a bug, how rude of me, sweet!
It mumbles a curse in a bug-like manner,
As I leap like a frog, the universe's planner!

Each moment a bubble, they rise and they pop,
In this carnival, I can't seem to stop.
With laughter and joy wrapped in a spin,
Oh, to be timeless, just let the fun in!

A Stream of Endless Moments

I dipped my toes in a river of giggles,
It splashed me back, oh, how it wriggles!
Fish were cracking jokes in the bright sunlight,
A catfish winked, making everything bright.

Floating downstream, I met a wise old toad,
He squabbled with the ducks in their silly abode.
"You think you're timeless?" he croaked with a grin,
"I'm the king of this stream; let the games begin!"

A leaf passed by, wearing a tiny hat,
It floated in circles while I sat with a spat.
"Where's my invitation?" I quipped to the breeze,
It just laughed and whispered, "Life's a tease."

With each splish and splash, I'm lost in the fun,
Time's just a trickster, playing 'hide and run.'
From moments to memories, I stream along,
With laughter and joy, this life's where I belong!

The Ocean of Infinite Reflections

In waves of laughter, wise fish sing,
They wear hats of seaweed, it's quite the thing.
They practice their jokes in coral cafes,
While jellyfish giggle in floating ballets.

A crab with a monocle gives it a whirl,
Telling tall tales, he gives them a twirl.
Sea turtles are grooving to some funky beats,
While octopuses dance with eight happy feet.

The seashells all gather, they're keen on a chat,
About seasickness woes and a lost sailor's hat.
They chuckle and shimmer under sun's glow,
In a splashy parade where all sea creatures go.

Unraveled Threads of Time

In the weaving of hours, socks disappear,
A mystery wrapped in the fabric of cheer.
Time ticks in circles, just like a clock,
While moments get tangled in quite the big shock.

A ribbon of seconds, now frayed at the edge,
Sends butterflies flying to make a strange pledge.
Old hats talk gossip, with whispers of flair,
About how the cat's got the treadmill to spare.

Chasing lost minutes is their favorite game,
With clocks that run backward, they all take the blame.
They laugh at the chaos, don't mind the sprawl,
In this closet of time, we're all having a ball.

The Celestial Flow

Stars prance in the night, twinkling with glee,
Making wishes on comets, as bright as can be.
A moon made of cheese, with a smile so wide,
Can't stop cracking jokes as it does its moon slide.

Galaxies giggle, their laughter like light,
As planets play tag in the velvety night.
UFOs are teachers of funny old lore,
While aliens laugh till they roll on the floor.

Constellations gather for cosmic ballet,
Dancing with meteorites, hip-hip hooray!
In this endless sky, there's always much more,
As we float in this humor, forever we score.

Ever-Expanding Horizons

Horizons are stretching, like dough on a plate,
As pancakes flip over, it's hard to celebrate.
Birds in bowties are taking the lead,
With dreams of tall trees where they plant laughter seeds.

Each sunrise a joke, so fresh and so bright,
They gather in laughter, from day until night.
The clouds wear their hats, puffed up and so proud,
While thunder claps jokes in a booming loud crowd.

Adventures await in the land down below,
Where laughter is currency and giggles will grow.
With every new dawn, there's a tale to be told,
As horizons keep bending, becoming more bold.

Threads Between the Now and Never

In a world where socks lose their pairs,
Time trips over little chairs.
We laugh as seconds skip and hop,
While clocks just dance and never stop.

A cat that thinks it's a time machine,
Chasing dust motes, oh what a scene!
It pounces on the past and future,
With the grace of a furry tutor.

We wear our watches on our feet,
Counting moments, oh so sweet.
But they just tick in silly ways,
And pause to laugh at lazy days.

So here we play with a jester's glee,
Untangling yarn from reality.
Each thread we pull creates a jest,
In this tapestry, we find our rest.

Beyond the Shores of Defined Time

Where moments drift like boats in the breeze,
We trade our clocks for cups of cheese.
The minutes laugh as they slip away,
And leap into tomorrow's play.

Time serves ice cream in a cone,
With sprinkles made of ancient bone.
If you blink, you'll miss a star,
So dive right in, don't stay ajar!

We build sandcastles from old seconds,
With jokes that break all time's reckonings.
Laughter echoes in each grain,
As we frolic in this merry lane.

So set your sails, let us glide,
On waves where whimsy, not dread, resides.
Together we'll sail, till time is naught,
With giggles and grins, and all that's sought.

Flight of the Endless River

A river flows with winks and grins,
Carrying whispers and silly sins.
It bubbles with laughter, splashes delight,
With fish that dance under the moonlight.

As it swirls through the fields of jest,
Carrying dreams past the sun's bright nest.
It tickles the toes of the playful breeze,
And rolls in waves like a clown's tease.

Time takes a plunge, makes a cannonball,
Squirting splashes, conquering all.
The sun wears shades; the stars just chase,
As the river laughs, leaving no trace.

So hop on a leaf, float with the rill,
In this current, our hearts find thrill.
We're all just fish in a whimsical stream,
Riding the wave of a joyous dream.

The Dance of Timeless Spirits

Spirits twirl in a phantom show,
With whimsical hats and a bright green glow.
They laugh as they leap through the walls of fate,
With cha-chas and waltzes, oh isn't it great?

They throw a party in the midnight air,
Balloons that giggle and do the flair.
A tuba plays tunes that tickle your toes,
While the moon winks brightly, everyone knows.

In their dance of silliness, time takes flight,
Each leap and twirl makes the stars feel light.
They twist and turn with jokes and tricks,
Crafting memories, handing out kicks.

So join the dance, let rhythm unfold,
With timeless spirits, in joy be bold.
For laughter is the song we all adore,
In this dance of life, forevermore.

The String of Timelessness

In a place where clocks hang upside down,
Tick-tock's lost, a silly frown.
Time dances, jumps, and skips around,
Wearing pajamas, it never gets found.

Each second slips on a banana peel,
With giggles echoing, it's quite the deal.
Time has no hurry, it strolls with flair,
Wearing a top hat and an old teddy bear.

Days twirl like pasta on a fork,
Silly shadows come out to talk.
They gossip 'bout things that never do change,
Like the soup that always tastes a bit strange.

In the string of moments, we giggle so bright,
Chasing rainbows and fuzzy things in flight.
Forever's a prankster, a playful tease,
In this laughter-filled world, we do as we please.

Across the Sea of Eternity

Sailing on a ship made of giggles and glee,
Chasing waves that dance just for me.
Seashells whisper secrets in a silly tone,
As seagulls wear sunglasses, blinged like a throne.

The horizon smiles with a cheeky grin,
Telling tales of jellybeans that spin.
Fish in bow ties swim with pride,
In this wacky ocean, magic won't hide.

Stars dive into the water for a splash,
While the moon does a waltz, oh what a bash!
Clouds wear flippers and float on by,
Singing tunes with a wink and a sigh.

With every wave, the laughter flows,
Tickling feet of all the crows.
Across the sea, where time is a joke,
We dance on the waves in our laughter cloak.

Unseen Waves of Existence

In a pond where ripples hum a tune,
Frogs wear hats that reflect the moon.
Invisible waves play hide and seek,
While turtles break dance, oh so unique!

A chuckle floats in the air like mist,
Waves of laughter that cannot be missed.
Socks swim upstream while shoes take a dive,
In this wild place, all sillies thrive.

Time hula-hoops on a breeze so light,
Chasing clouds as they tease and fright.
Gentle nudges from a breeze's hand,
Send us spinning in this wacky land.

Each moment's a party, fresh and new,
Sipping gigs from silly straws, who knew?
With unseen waves, we bounce and sway,
Laughing together, come what may.

Harmonies of the Everdivine

In a symphony of giggles, sweet and loud,
The universe dances, oh so proud.
Stars chuckle, notes flapping in flight,
Drifting in melodies guiding the night.

The moon's in a chorus, happy and bright,
Cuddling the sun, what a joyful sight.
Clouds play the drums, quick and unsure,
With rhythms of laughter, so pure!

Harmony sings while shadows play darts,
As time taps its feet to joyful arts.
We sway in the breeze, a delicate spin,
In the world of the funny, we twist and grin.

The echoes of joy shimmer in the air,
In each silly note, love is laid bare.
Together, we laugh in this sweet serenade,
In the dance of existence, we won't be swayed.

Boundless Ripples

With socks on feet, we leap and spin,
Making waves of laughter, let the fun begin.
Chasing dreams like bubbles in the air,
Each giggle echoing, without a care.

Time's a tricky jester with a snicker,
As we dance along, our steps get quicker.
We ride on whims, like ducks in a pond,
Splashing joy as endless as a magic wand.

Lollygagging through sunlit days,
Beneath the sun's mischievous rays.
Building castles from sand and foam,
Finding treasure in every giddy roam.

So let's twirl in this delight, my friend,
Where laughter echoes, it never must end.
With each tickle of time, let's delight in play,
As we spin through the smirk of each new day.

Journeying Through the Infinite

We ride on rainbows, spiraling high,
Where unicorns giggle and time likes to fly.
Chasing our shadows with silly little hops,
In this wild adventure, we never must stop.

Each twinkling star winks, giving a cheer,
As cupcakes rain down, oh what a sphere!
We dodge the mundane with each epic leap,
While giggling into the abyss, not a peep.

In the land of the lost things, we search for a sock,
Befriending dust bunnies, we'll take them for a walk.
Come on, let's skip on the clouds made of cream,
Where silliness reigns and giggles do beam.

So onward we scoot, on marshmallow ships,
Navigating laughter with banana peel dips.
With every layer of joy, we unwrap life's fun,
In this adventure, we'll never be done.

Tides of the Eternal Sea

We paddle in puddles like sharks in a stew,
With fishing rods made of candy, woo-hoo!
Seagulls squawk tricks at our froggy ballet,
As we boat on the waves, oh what a display!

The tides pull us closer like a comedic dance,
While we pirouette in our splashy romance.
Barnacles gossip, sharing the lore,
Of clams doing cartwheels on the ocean's floor.

Splashing about with jellyfish pals,
Trading silly stories from seaweed gals.
Whales hum lullabies, oh so bizarre,
In this watery realm, we're absolute stars!

So let's surf through giggles as we glide with glee,
Riding waves of laughter, wild and free.
With every ripple, our hearts bloom and swell,
In this whimsical world, we're under a spell.

The Labyrinth of Timelessness

In a maze of giggles, we wander and roam,
Finding paths lined with candy, calling us home.
Every twist and turn, a laugh or a cheer,
We meet silly squirrels, full of good cheer.

Where the clocks are all melted like ice cream in sun,
And seconds fly by, oh isn't this fun?
We map out our giggles, we calculate joy,
Navigating nonsense, our favorite ploy.

The corridors wiggle, with rubbery bends,
Hiding tickling secrets and jelly-bean friends.
As we skip through this riddle with bubbling delight,
Time's just an illusion, a whimsy in flight.

So let's dance in this puzzle where laughter's the guide,
In this silly escapade, let your heart open wide.
In the labyrinth of joy, where we play without end,
Every moment is magic, my dear, my dear friend.

The Eternal Ripple

A pebble falls, a splash ignites,
Fish flip and swirl, giving me fright.
I try to play it oh so cool,
But end up as a soggy fool.

The frogs croak songs of absolute joy,
While I sit here, my dreams they'll toy.
A ripple spreads, the ducks take flight,
Do I join in? Or stay out of sight?

The water winks, it's got some sass,
"Jump on in, don't let it pass!"
So here I go, a splash and a grin,
What's a little soaking? Let the fun begin!

Each wave a giggle, each splash a cheer,
I'd stay forever, if I could, my dear.
Hopping like a frog, I make my mark,
In this pond of laughs, I'm the lark!

Dance of Infinite Currents

The sea sways as if to tease,
Tickling the shores with playful ease.
Seagulls dance a crazy salsa,
While I awkwardly try to salsa.

Wave after wave, a flow so grand,
I toss my chips, they shift like sand.
"My fortune's here!" I shout with glee,
But seagulls think it's snacks for free!

Fish are laughing in their finned delight,
As I do the crab walk, what a sight!
The ocean laughs, the sun a bright pin,
Who knew my dance moves could cause such a din?

With tides changing like my mood each day,
I waddle on the beach, come what may.
Splashing merrily, my steps a ballet,
In this infinite rhythm, I shall stay!

Chasing Yesterday's Tomorrow

With a cup of coffee, dreams unfurl,
I trip on my shoelace; what a whirl!
Yesterday's thoughts are riding the breeze,
But my pants are stuck like a stubborn tease.

Every tick of the clock's a little race,
I'm late for a meeting, oh what a disgrace!
Running in circles, my mind on a spree,
Chasing my past just to lose my tea!

I glance at the sky, clouds start to giggle,
I stumble and fumble, doing the wiggle.
Tomorrow's right there, but I'm stuck on today,
Maybe I'll nap, and sleep my cares away!

But the sun peeks through with a glittery grin,
"Stop chasing shadows; let the fun begin!"
So I chase the laughter, not worry or dread,
In this silly dance, joy's truly widespread!

Unbroken Waves

There's a rhythm to life, they say,
But I'm just a bumblebee in a ballet.
My dance is chaotic, a curious sway,
Like waves in a storm, I'm lost in the fray.

The tide rolls in with a cheeky smirk,
It whispers, "Relax, you silly jerk!"
I think it knows my every misstep,
As I channel my inner water adept.

The beach umbrellas flap like they're mad,
While I splash water, attempting to clad.
A surfer zooms by, waves my way,
But I just float along, come what may!

"Unbroken waves," I hear the ocean claim,
As I giggle and shout, "Hey, I'm the same!"
So here in my towel, I will forever stay,
Finding joy in this dance, come what may!

The Ocean of Always

A fish wore a hat, what a sight,
He swam with delight, in the moonlight.
With every wave, he'd crack a grin,
Saying, "Life's a joke, let the laughter begin!"

The jellyfish danced, with a twirl and sway,
They laughed at the crabs who got in their way.
The seaweed giggled, tickling the toes,
In a world full of fun, anything goes!

A dolphin appeared, in a bright tutu,
"I'm off to the party, won't you join too?"
We'll ride on the waves, till the break of dawn,
Making silly faces, till the laughter is gone!

So dive in the fun, let your worries flee,
In this ocean of joy, you'll be wild and free.
With friends all around, it's a comical spree,
In laughter we swim, as happy as can be!

Timeless Ripples

In a pond so round, a frog takes a leap,
With a big goofy grin, it's making us weep.
He croaks out a tune, with notes all askew,
Even the fish join in, humming along too!

The sun shines bright, on a cloud made of fluff,
While ducks in a row quack, "We're tough enough!"
They paddle and wobble, pretending to race,
What a hilarious sight, with that silly duck face!

A turtle on floaties, just soaking in rays,
Shouting, "I'm the king of these carefree days!"
While a beetle on skates gives the crowd quite a show,
Everyone's laughing at the moves that he'll throw!

As ripples expand, spreading chuckles around,
Life's punchlines and giggles in circles abound.
In this timeless dance, with joy we'll croon,
So let's keep on laughing, 'neath the sun and the moon!

A Dance with Infinity

In a land of odd shapes, where time does cartwheels,
A cat wearing socks declares, "This is how it feels!"
The clocks all tick tock in a jazzy old tune,
With every silly moment, they hop to the moon!

A thousand balloons, each with a grin,
Float off to the sky, where fun times begin.
They dance in the breeze, twirling here and there,
With laughter so loud, you'd think it's unfair!

An octopus juggles, with arms all around,
While a squirrel in shades spins, bursting with sound.
They laugh at the stars, who wink back with glee,
In this wild party where all can be free!

So twirl 'round with glee, let your worries take flight,
In this dance of the ages, every moment's delight.
We'll giggle and wiggle, until the day's end,
In a fiesta of laughter that time will suspend!

Threads of Unbroken Time

In a tapestry woven, of giggles and cheer,
A rabbit in glasses said, "Life is quite dear!"
He threaded through jokes, making stitches of fun,
With each little pun, the whole world was won!

The buttons were dancing, each twirl was a blast,
Singing, "We're stuck here, but we're having a vast!"
A needle popped in, with a wink and a grin,
Saying, "Let's get this going, the fun has begun!"

A measuring tape stretched, as far as it could,
Yelling, "Let's capture all this laughter for good!"
And the scissors just snipped, with a snicker and rhyme,
Chopping off worries, unbinding our time!

So gather your threads, let's stitch up some smiles,
In this quilt of hilarity, spanning for miles.
With a sew and a quilt, let joy intertwine,
In the fabric of laughter, where our hearts brightly shine!

The Rhythm of Never-Ending

I danced with squirrels, pranced with glee,
But tripped on my shoelace—oh, woe is me!
Coffee gone cold, the toast took flight,
In the chaos of morning, I lost my sight.

Tick tock goes the clock in a silly race,
Time laughs at me, it's not a kind face.
I juggle my woes like a clown with a grin,
But somehow I always trip over my chin.

My cat thinks he's king, but a jester he'll stay,
His royal decree: ignore all the play!
I chase him around with a feathered stick,
But in his grand scheme, he's just too quick.

Yet here's to the moments that tickle my soul,
Where laughter and folly make life feel whole.
As I waddle through life in a dance quite absurd,
I find joy in the jests, oh, haven't you heard?

Veins of Ageless Water

Beneath the surface, fish wear a grin,
They gossip in bubbles about where to swim.
A turtle named Ted boasts how fast he can crawl,
But everyone knows he just likes to stall.

Raindrops play poker on the window ledge,
Betting their futures, it's quite the edge.
The clouds make a pact, they'll rain down on me,
But I just wanted sunshine—oh, can't they see?

Puddles become mirrors for ducks in a row,
Quacking their wisdom, they all steal the show.
And when the sun sets in a splash of pink,
I ponder if fish ever stop to think.

Oh, life's a wet fest in this watery spree,
Where even the drizzles dance wild and free.
So let's splash through the hours, let worries unfurl,
For in each little droplet, the world's quite a whirl!

Unfurling the Eternal Flow

A leaf whispered secrets to the buzzing bee,
While a worm on a leaf was busy with tea.
Twisting and rolling like they'd won the race,
Spouting their wisdom in a leafy embrace.

The wind made a ruckus, a wild, breezy jest,
It tickled the branches and played with the best.
A crow wore a hat, quite dapper and neat,
Declaring that worms were the best kind of treat.

The squirrels held meetings, planning great schemes,
On how to outsmart the humans, it seems.
With acorns for ammunition, they plotted and planned,
But dropped all their snacks—oh, isn't life grand?

So revel in nature's funny ballet,
Where critters take center stage, come what may.
Each chuckle of wind, every tickle of grass,
Is proof we all laugh, as the moments just pass.

Currents Beneath a Starry Sky

Stars waltz and twirl in a glittery dance,
While I trip on the sidewalk, lost in a trance.
The moonlit path whispers, "Watch where you go,"
But I'm too busy dreaming, just putting on a show.

Owls provide commentary, wise and sly,
They hoot out my blunders as I tumble by.
A raccoon in a mask sneaks a peek, quite distraught,
At my epic fails—if only they could be caught!

Fireflies blink messages, all coded in light,
I wave my hands wildly, "Is this day or night?"
While shadows participate in a game of charades,
I'm left in their dust, in celestial cascades.

But under this sky, with laughter abound,
I find in my fumbles, some joy can be found.
So let's cherish the clumsy, embrace the absurd,
For even missteps can sing, if we've truly heard!

Unraveling the Fabric of Now

Stitching time with threads of glee,
I tripped on the future, oh woe is me!
My alarm clock dances like a cat on fire,
Lost in a dream, I twist and tire.

With coffee cups that never seem to fill,
I juggle minutes, but they're far from still.
Each second a clown, a laugh so bright,
In this circus of now, everything's a fright.

Time's a jester with tricks up its sleeve,
Pulling pranks on poor souls like me who believe.
I chase after moments, but they flee like sprites,
Caught in the whirlwind of mundane delights.

But hey, I'm just here having a hoot,
As reality's rubbery, that's how we scoot!
With a wink and a nod, let's dance through the haze,
In this fabric of now, we'll be lost in a maze!

Embrace of the Ever-Now

Tick-tock goes the clock, what a sneaky beast,
It claims to be constant, but it's quite the feast.
In pajamas of moments, I prance with grace,
Dancing in circles, can't find my place.

Oh, the present's a party, a revel not planned,
With party hats made of procrastination's hand.
I toast to the chaos, and laugh with delight,
While time throws confetti, it's a glorious sight!

I reached for tomorrow but bumped my own head,
Got tangled in "now" and fell out of bed.
But why should I worry, or even fret,
When life is a joke that I haven't quite met?

So here's to the moment, let's give it a cheer,
With each giggle and chuckle, we'll conquer the year.
In this embrace of the goofy and bright,
Let's waltz with the sundown, it feels just right!

Voyage Through Endless Waters

Set sail on a puddle, my tiny brigade,
In boats made of paper, our daring escapade.
We'll paddle through raindrops, glide on a whim,
In this ocean of nonsense, our laughter won't dim.

The horizon's a donut, sweet and divine,
With sprinkles of whimsy, let's have a good time.
Oh look, a fish wearing spectacles too,
He winked and he giggled, said, "Hey, how are you?"

I found a lost sock, it said "Aye Aye, mate!"
Claiming the tides have been rather late.
With waves made of jelly, we surf on the goo,
Finding treasures of giggles, and silly sea stew.

So hoist up the humour, and let's ride the waves,
For every splash echoes with laughter that saves.
In this voyage of jest, we'll sail evermore,
Through waters of light, and memories galore!

Celestial Streams

From star to star in a wobbly boat,
I paddled through cosmos, what a wild goat!
The moon wore a cap, said, "Oh dear, oh me!"
Winking down at my cosmic jubilee.

Asteroids giggle, they dance in a line,
While comets zoom past, drinking stardust wine.
I tossed them some jokes, they shimmered with glee,
Spinning tales of tomorrow, just you wait and see!

Nebulas stretch out like blankets of cheer,
A quilt of the universe, wrapped up in here.
With each twinkling star, life's a cosmic joke,
As I paddle through laughter, the universe pokes.

So let's race the starlight, and tease time apart,
For in this expanse lies a whimsical heart.
In these celestial streams, we'll frolic and play,
In a galaxy filled with giggles, we'll drift away!

Perpetual Horizons

Onward we sail, like ants on a spree,
Chasing our dreams while sipping sweet tea.
Time tickles us gently, what a grand jest,
As we dance through the ages, we're truly the best!

Watch as the clocks take a tumble and fall,
They giggle and wobble, then stand proud and tall.
Life in a loop, what a rollercoaster ride,
With giggles and snorts, we gladly abide!

As stars wink their eyes in the cosmic ballet,
We moonwalk through eons, let's dance here and sway.
The sun slips a joke while it warms up the pond,
We laugh at the shadows that we've somehow conned!

Oh, the crunch of the cosmos, what a tasty delight,
Nibbling on comets under a blanket of night.
With playful revolutions, we twirl and we spin,
In this dizzying ride where the fun will begin!

The Pulse of Eons

Tick-tock, the universe plays peek-a-boo,
With planets in costumes, how silly, who knew?
Time wears a wig that's all frizzy and wild,
It's a soap opera plot, oh how we've been beguiled!

The moon serves popcorn in its cratered abode,
While meteors zip by, flashing their code.
They wink and they chuckle at our earthly plight,
As we trip over timelines in ticklish delight!

Racing through ages on a pogo stick,
With history and humor, we dance to the tick.
Elves in the forest ride unicorns fast,
In the playful embrace of a time that won't last!

We juggle the past as the future rolls in,
Making prank calls to fate, let the games now begin.
With laughter like echoes through nebulous days,
Life is a funny business in so many ways!

An Everlasting Voyage

Set sail on a ship made of giggles and light,
We navigate whimsies, what a curious sight!
Stars line up neatly, ready to cheer,
Come join our parade, we'll have fun all year!

With each gentle wave, it's a whoopee cushion,
As time flies us onward in playful confusion.
A compass that points to the nearest punchline,
We journey through laughter, oh isn't it fine?

Cartwheeling comets spill jokes from afar,
They whisper sweet nothings, "You're a shining star!"
Ride rainbows of giggles, let's soar through the skies,
What a whimsical trip, with no need for goodbyes!

Anchors aren't needed, we float ever free,
With whimsy and antics, we'll always agree.
So hold onto your hats, it's a ride beyond measure,
In this voyage of joy, we're boundless in pleasure!

Bound in Stream and Time

Floating like ducks in a puddle divine,
We paddle through moments, how ludicrously fine!
Rippling with laughter, we swirl round the bend,
Each second a giggle, each hour a friend.

The river of nonsense flows oh-so-sweet,
We toss in our worries, watch them retreat.
With turtles on skateboards and fish that can sing,
This whimsical stream sure gives time a good fling!

Lollipop lilies bloom in perfect array,
Where time turns to gumdrops and demands for play.
We skip on the currents, with joy filling our sails,
As mermaids and mirth ride on whimsical tales!

So let's keep on splashing in this babbling groove,
With moments of laughter, we'll endlessly move.
In streams of delight where the fun intertwines,
We're bound in the laughter that sweetly defines!

www.ingramcontent.com/pod-product-compliance
Lightning Source LLC
Chambersburg PA
CBHW060127230426
43661CB00003B/354